Introduction

This book is not only about rice.

Here are 30 recipes in which the ingredients include rice (in some recipes, rice will be the main ingredient, and in some will be addition to the dish)

Most often you will encounter exotic dishes that are often found in China, Thailand, Japan, etc.

I hope this book will bring you new sensations!

Bon appetite !

EASY SUSHI ROLLS

- *PREP TIME:* ONE HOUR

- *PREPARE TIME:* 0 MINS

- *TOTAL TIME:* ONE HOUR

- *YIELD:* APPROXIMATELY 5 ROLLS (40 PIECES)

INGREDIENTS
- 1 batch sushi rice (next recipe), cooled to approximately 25 °C
- 5 sheets nori
- 1 English cucumber, sliced in thin strips
- 2 avocados, peeled, pitted and sliced in thin strips
- ten ounces smoked salmon either sushi-grade raw fish, sliced in thin strips
- toasted sesame seeds
- spicy mayo *(see recipe below)*
- soy sauce, pickled ginger and wasabi paste, for submitting

INSTRUCTIONS
1. **Prep all of your ingredients.** It's significant to have all of your ingredients prepped and ready to go *before* you begin to assemble your rolls. (I especially advised cooking the rice 1-two hours ahead of time, so that this can cool to approximately 25 °C before assembling the rolls.)
2. **Put the rice. place** a sheet of nori on a sushi mat* smooth-side-down, with the longer side of the nori facing you. Place a bowl of water nearby. Dip your fingers in the water (this can help the rice not to stick) and strew approximately one cup of sushi rice evenly over the nori, leaving a 1-inch border open at the top. employing your fingers, carefully however firmly Put the rice onto the nori in some even layer, dipping your fingers back in the water as often as needed so that they Dont stick. You want the rice to overlay the nori as evenly as probable, all the way to the down, left and right edges of the sheet. (See photos above.)

3. **Add the fillings.** Place the fillings in long horizontal lines on top of the rice, layering the different fillings side by side instead of in one big pile. Strew the toppings a pinch of sesame seeds, supposing desired.

4. **Roll up the sushi.** Lift up the down edge of the sushi mat and attentively place down this over the fillings till they are enclosed in a roll, yet still leaving the top 1-inch of the empty nori exposed. employthe sushi mat to squeeze the roll in as tightly as probable. (Although not *too* tight, as you don't want all of the fillings to squish out!) Dip your fingers within the water bowl as more and employthem to wet the remaining 1-inch of nori. Then employthe sushi mat to finish rolling up the roll till this is completely enclosed. Give this a several extra squeezes all around so that this is good and firmly-packed. Then Place the entire roll to a cutting board. recur with the remaining ingredients to form approximately 5 sushi rolls.

5. **Slice the sushi. employing** a very sharp knife, slice the every sushi roll in 8 equal(ish)-sized pieces. Place them to your submitting plate.

6. **Drizzle and garnish.** Drizzle the sushi with the spicy mayo and/or strew with extra toasted sesame seeds.

7. **Serve. submit** immediately, along with pickled ginger, wasabi paste, and soy gravy for dipping. And enjoy!

NOTES

Spicy mayo: blend along One-quarter cup Japanese mayo (or any kind of mayo either plain Greek yogurt) and 4 tsps sriracha sauce till mixd. Taste and place extra sriracha supposing you would like a spicier sauce. (You'll also place in a tiny drizzle of toasted sesame oil and/or honey, supposing desired.) I like to drizzle the mayo on top of the rolls simply before submitting, however you'll also blend this in with the fillings instead.

SUSHI RICE

- *PREP TIME:* 5 MINS

- *PREPARE TIME:* 30 MINS

- *TOTAL TIME:* 35 MINS

- *YIELD:* APPROXIMATELY 4 CUPS

INGREDIENTS
- 2 cups Japanese short-grain rice ("sushi rice")
- 2 cups water
- 4-inch square of kombu *(if you want)*
- One-quarter cup unseasoned rice vinegar
- 4 tsps sugar *(or honey)*
- 1 tsp fine sea salt

INSTRUCTIONS
1. **Rinse the rice.** Rinse the rice with cold water in a big fine mesh strainer for 1-2 mins, either till the water runs very clear. Drain good.
2. **Cook the rice.** See details within the notes below for how to prepare the rice either on the stovetop, in a rice cooker, either within the Instant Pot.
3. **Make the sushi vinegar.** Whereas the rice is cooking, warmth the rice vinegar, sugar and sea salt along in a small saucepan over average-high warmth till the mix nearly reaches a simmer. Take away from warmth and blend till the sugar has dissolved. (Alternately, you'll simply warmth the mix within the microwave supposing you prefer.)
4. **Spice the rice.** As the rice is cooked, Place the rice instantly to a big mixing bowl and drizzle this evenly with the sushi vinegar. employ a spatula to very carefully place down the rice — more of a slicing and lifting motion, rather than mixing and smooshing — till the vinegar is evenly mixed in the rice.
5. **Cool.** Overlay the mixing bowl with a damp towel so that this is touching the surface of the rice, which can help prevent the rice from

drying out. allow this cool on the counter (or within the refrigerator) till this reaches approximately 25 °C.

6. **Serve. employ**the rice instantly in a recipe, either Place to some airtight food storage container and refrigerate for up to 3 days.

NOTES

Rice Cooker Instructions: Shortstir the rice and water along within the bowl of a rice cooker, then place the kombu on top of the rice. Overlay and prepare therefore to device instructions. Discard the kombu.

Instant Pot **Instructions:** Shortstir the rice and water along within the bowl of some Instant Pot, then place the kombu on top of the rice. Overlay and Puture prepare on high for 5 mins, followed by a ten minute natural release, followed by a quick release. Discard the kombu.

Stovetop Instructions: Shortstir along the rice and water (I advised employing two One-quarter cups water for this method) in a big saucepan, place the kombu on top of the rice, then overlay the saucepan with a tight-fitting lid. Turn the warmth to average-high and prepare till the water *simply* reaches a simmer. Decrease warmth to average-low to maintain the simmer, and prepare for 16-18 mins either till all of the liquid is absorbed and the rice is tender. Take away saucepan from the warmth (with the lid still on) and allow the rice steam for some additional ten mins. Discard the kombu.

SESAME CHICKEN SALAD

- *PREP TIME:* **20 MINS**

- *PREPARE TIME:* **0 MINS**

- *TOTAL TIME:* **20 MINS**

- *YIELD:* **4-6 SUBMITTINGS**

INGREDIENTS

SALAD INGREDIENTS:

- 1 (14-ounce) bag coleslaw *(or 7 cups shredded cabbage)*
- 2 cups diced either shredded prepared chicken
- one cup loosely-packed sliced cilantro
- 2/3 cup sliced green onions
- 2/3 cup sliced either slivered almonds, toasted
- half cup shredded carrots
- 1 avocado, peeled, pitted and diced
- toasted sesame seeds, for sprinkling.

SESAME VINAIGRETTE INGREDIENTS:

- 2 tbsp avocado oil *(or olive oil)*
- 2 tbsp rice vinegar
- 1 tbsp low-sodium soy sauce *(or tamari)*
- 1 tbsp maple syrup either honey
- 1 tsp toasted sesame oil
- half tsp ground ginger
- 1 small garlic clove, Puted either minced *(or One-quarter tsp garlic powder)*
- a several twists of freshly-cracked black pepper

INSTRUCTIONS

1. **Make the vinaigrette: blend** along all ingredients in a small bowl (or shake along in a mason jar) till mixd.
2. **Toss the** <u>salad</u>**:** Mix the coleslaw, <u>chicken</u>, cilantro, green onions, almonds, carrots and avocado togehter in a big mixing bowl, drizzle with the vinaigrette, and toss till mixd
3. **Serve: submit** the <u>salad</u> immediately, sprinkled with sesame seeds as a garnish.

CHICKEN AND WILD RICE SOUP

- *PREP TIME:* TEN MINS

- *PREPARE TIME:* 50 MINS

- *TOTAL TIME:* ONE HOUR

- *YIELD:* 6-8 SUBMITTINGS

INGREDIENTS

- 2 tbsp butter either olive oil
- 1 small white either yellow onion, peeled and diced
- 2 average carrots, diced
- 2 celery stalks, diced
- 6 cloves garlic, minced
- One-quarter cup all-purpose flour
- 6 cups chicken stock *(or veggie stock)*
- 1 pound boneless skinless chicken breasts*
- 8 ounces baby bella mushrooms, diced
- one cup unprepared wild rice, rinsed and drained
- 1 tbsp finely-sliced fresh rosemary
- 2 bay leaves
- 2 cups plain milk *(cow's milk either plant-based milk)*
- 2 big handfuls fresh baby spinach, roughly sliced
- fine sea salt and freshly-cracked black pepper

INSTRUCTIONS

1. **Sauté the veggies. soften** butter either oil in a big stockpot over average-high heat. place onion and sauté for 4 mins, mixing sometimes. place carrots, celery and garlic and sauté for 3 more mins, mixing sometimes. place within the flour and sauté for one more minute, mixing frequently.
2. **Add within the next round of ingredients.** Gradually pour within the chicken stock, mixing the soup frequently as you pour so that the clumps

of flour can soften in the broth. place the chicken breasts, mushrooms, wild rice, rosemary, bay leaves and stir to mix.

3. **Simmer. allow** the soup keep cooking till this reaches a simmer. Then decrease warmth to average-low to maintain the simmer, cover, and prepare for 40-45 mins either till the wild rice is tender — being sure to stir the soup every 5-7 mins so that the down of the pot does not burn.

4. **Shred either dice the** chicken. **employ**tongs to attentively Place the chicken breasts to a clear plate. Then you'll either dice either employtwo forks to shred the chicken in bite-sized pieces, and stir this back in the soup.

5. **Add the remaining ingredients.** Stir within the milk and baby spinach till mixd.

6. **Season.** Take away and discard the bay leaves. Taste and spice the soup with however much salt and black pepper you think this needs.

7. **Serve. submit** warm and enjoy!

NOTES

Chicken**: either** feel free to place in 3-4 cups of (precooked) diced either shredded chicken instead of raw chicken.

Instant Pot **Option:** To prepare Puture cooker chicken and wild rice soup, simply place the onion, carrots, celery, garlic, chicken stock, chicken breasts, wild rice, rosemary and bay leaves to the bowl of your Instant Pot. Cover, seal and prepare on high Puture for 30 mins, followed by a ten minute natural release, followed by a quick release. Meanwhereas in a else saucepan, warmth the butter over average-high warmth till softened. blend within the flour till mixd and prepare for one minute, mixing frequently. Then blend within the milk till mixd and keep heating till the mix thickens. Take away from warmth and place the mix to the soup. Keep on with steps 4-7.

Crock-Pot Option: To prepare slow cooker chicken and wild rice soup, simply place the onion, carrots, celery, garlic, chicken stock, chicken breasts, wild rice, rosemary and bay leaves to the bowl of a big slow cooker. Overlay and prepare on high for 3-4 hours either on poor for 6-8 hours, till the rice is tender. Meanwhereas in a else saucepan, warmth the butter over average-high warmth till softened. blend within the flour till mixd and prepare for one minute, mixing frequently. Then blend within the milk till mixd and keep heating till the mix thickens. Take away from warmth and place the mix to the soup. Keep on with steps 4-7.

KOREAN STEAK BOWLS

- *PREP TIME:* **25 MINS**

- *PREPARE TIME:* **5 MINS**

- *TOTAL TIME:* **30 MINS**

- *YIELD:* **4-6 SUBMITTINGS**

INGREDIENTS

STEAK BITES:

- 1 half pounds flank steak, slice in 1-inch cubes
- fine sea salt and freshly-cracked black pepper
- 1 tbsp avocado oil *(or any high-warmth oil)*
- 1–2 tbsp low-sodium soy sauce

SESAME CUCUMBER SLAW:

- 1 (14-ounce) bag coleslaw
- 1 English cucumber, sliced in half moons
- one cup sliced fresh cilantro
- 2/3 cup thinly-sliced green onions
- 2 tbsp rice vinegar
- 1 tbsp low-sodium soy sauce
- 1 tbsp maple syrup
- 1 tbsp toasted sesame oil
- if you want: two tsps toasted sesame seeds

SPICY SAUCE:

- one-third cup plain Greek yogurt *(or mayo)*
- 2 tbsp gochujang paste

RICE:

- 1 half cups white either brown rice

INSTRUCTIONS

1. **Cook the rice. prepare** the rice therefore to package instructions.
2. **Make the** <u>sauce</u>**: blend** along the Greek yogurt and gochujang till mixd. Supposing you would like to turn the gravy in more of a drizzly <u>dressing</u>, blend in a several extra tbsp of water till the blend reaches your desired consistency. (And supposing this tastes a bit too spicy for your liking, stir in some extra Greek yogurt.)
3. **Make the slaw:** Toss all ingredients along in a big bowl till mixd.
4. **Cook the steak bites:** Spice the steak evenly with a generous pinch of salt and a several twists of freshly-cracked black pepper. Warmth the oil in a big sauté pan over high warmth till this is shimmering. (You want the pan to be very hot!) Quickly place the steak bites to the pan in some even layer. (Supposing your pan is too small for the steak bites to fit in a single layer, I advised cooking this in two batches.) prepare the steak for two mins without stirring. Then flip and prepare for 2-ish more mins, either till the steak is seared on both sides and prepared to your desired level of doneness. Place steak to a clear bowl and toss with the soy <u>sauce</u>.
5. **Assemble the bowls:** In your submitting bowls, stratum a portion of rice, slaw, and steak bites. Then drizzle generously with the spicy <u>sauce</u>, plus some if you want extra strew of sliced cilantro for garnish. Enjoy!

VEGAN PHO (VIETNAMESE NOODLE SOUP)

INGREDIENTS

PHO BOUILLON INGREDIENTS:

- 1 big white onion, peeled and halved
- 3-inch piece of fresh ginger, halved lengthwise
- 5 star anise
- 4 whole cloves
- 3 (3-inch) cinnamon sticks
- 2 cardamom pods
- 1 tbsp whole coriander seeds
- 8 cups good-quality vegetable stock *(or mushroom stock*)*
- 1 tbsp brown sugar
- 2 tsps low-sodium soy gravy either tamari
- 2 tsps rice vinegar
- fine sea salt, to taste

PHO SOUP INGREDIENTS:

- 7 ounces unprepared thin rice noodles
- 1 tbsp olive oil *(or any neutral-flavored oil)*
- 8 ounces shiitake mushrooms, thinly sliced
- 2 heads baby bok choy, halved
- if you want: 1-2 cups extra veggies *(such as sliced carrots, broccoli florets, snow peas, etc.)*
- garnishes: fresh herbs (cilantro, mint, and/or Thai basil), bean sprouts, lime wedges, thinly-sliced chiles (Thai bird chiles either jalapeños), thinly-sliced onions (green onions either white onions), sauces (hoisin and/or sriracha)

INSTRUCTIONS

1. **Char the onions and ginger.** Turn the oven broiler to high, and place the baking rack approximately 8 inches away from the heating elements. Place the onion and ginger cut-side-up on a baking sheet, and brush with a little bit of oil. Broil for approximately 7-ten mins, till the tops of the onion and ginger are slightly charred. Take away and put aside.

2. **Prep the noodles.** Meanwhereas, as your bouillon is simmering, prepare the noodles separately al dente therefore to the package instructions. Drain in a strainer, then shortrinse the noodles with cold water to prevent them from continuing to cook. (I also advised tossing the noodles with a drizzle of oil — such as sesame oil — to prevent them from sticking.)

3. **Make the broth.** Meanwhereas, warmth the anise, cloves, cinnamon, cardamom and coriander to a big stock pot over average-high warmth for approximately 3 mins till fragrant. place within the charred onion, ginger, stock, and stir to mix. Keep cooking till the bouillon reaches a simmer. Then decrease warmth to average-low, overlay with a lid, and keep to simmer for at least 30 mins. Strain out (and discard) the onions, ginger and spices. Stir the brown sugar, soy gravy and rice vinegar in the hot broth. Then finally, taste and spice the bouillon with salt as needed. Keep simmering on average-low, covered, till ready to serve.

4. **Cook the veggies.** Meanwhereas, warmth the oil in a sauté pan over average-high heat. place the sliced mushrooms and sauté for 5 mins, mixing sometimes, till prepared through and slightly golden. Take away from heat. Then 5 mins before you are ready to submit the soup, stir the mushrooms, bok choy and veggies in the hot bouillon so that they can shortcook.

5. **Assemble.** And now…the fun part! place a handful of noodles to every individual submitting bowl. Ladle the hot bouillon and veggies in the submitting bowls. Top every bowl with lots and lots of garnishes, and finish with a generous squeeze of lime juice.

6. **Serve immediately.** Encouraging everyone to stir the garnishes in the soup so that they can flavor the broth, also adding in additional extra sauces supposing desired.

NOTES

- **Alternate mushroom option:** Supposing you would like to skip frying the mushrooms on the side, you are welcome to prepare them directly within the simmering bouillon itself. They must at least ten mins to cook, although the longer they simmer within there, the more delicious your bouillon can be.

- **Alternate charring option:** Instead of broiling the onion and ginger within the oven, you'll also simply prepare them cut-side-down in a sauté pan over high warmth till charred.

- **Double batch:** Again, I highly advised making a double batch of this recipe whereas you're at it! To do so, you'll must a big stockpot (at least 5 quarts) to handle the quantity of broth.

THAI CHICKEN WILD RICE SOUP

- *PREP TIME:* 15 MINS

- *PREPARE TIME:* 45 MINS

- *TOTAL TIME:* ONE HOUR

- *YIELD:* 6-8 SUBMITTINGS

INGREDIENTS

- 1 pound boneless skinless chicken breasts
- 8 ounces baby bella mushrooms, thinly sliced *(if you want)*
- 4 cloves garlic, minced
- 2 small bell peppers, diced *(I used one yellow, one red)*
- 2 average carrots, diced
- 1 small white either yellow onion, diced
- 6 cups chicken stock
- one cup unprepared wild rice
- 2 tbsp finely-sliced fresh ginger
- 2 tbsp Thai red curry paste
- 1 (15 ounce) can coconut milk
- garnishes: sliced fresh cilantro and fresh lime wedges

INSTRUCTIONS

INSTANT POT (PUTURE COOKER) INSTRUCTIONS:

1. Mix chicken, mushrooms, stock, garlic, bell peppers, carrots, onion, stock, wild rice, ginger and Thai chili paste within the bowl of some Instant Pot Puture cooker. Stir shortto mix.

2. Overlay and set vent to "sealing". prepare on manual (high Puture) for 30 mins. allow the Instant Pot rest for some extra ten mins (natural release). Then attentively turn the vent to "venting" and release the remaining Puture (quick release). Take away lid.

3. Place the prepared chicken to a else plate, and shred in bite-sized pieces with two forks.

4. Add the shredded chicken and coconut milk to the soup, and stir carefully till mixd. Taste and spice with salt, pepper and/or additional curry paste as needed.

5. Serve warm, garnished with cilantro and a squeeze of lime juice.

*CROCK-POT (**SLOW COOKER**) INSTRUCTIONS:*
1. Mix chicken, mushrooms, stock, garlic, bell peppers, carrots, onion, stock, wild rice, ginger and Thai chili paste within the bowl of a large slow cooker. Stir shortto mix, then overlay with a lid.
2. Cook on high for 3-4 hours either on poor for 6-8 hours, till the rice is tender and the chicken shreds simply.
3. Place the prepared chicken to a else plate, and shred in bite-sized pieces with two forks.

4. Add the shredded chicken and coconut milk to the soup, and stir carefully till mixd. Taste and spice with salt, pepper and/or additional curry paste as needed.

5. Serve warm, garnished with cilantro and a squeeze of lime juice.

STOVETOP INSTRUCTIONS:
1. Slice the chicken in small bite-sized pieces; put aside.

2. Warmth (an extra) one tbsp oil in a large stockpot over average-high heat. place onion and sauté for 5 mins, mixing sometimes, till soft and translucent. Stir within the garlic and ginger and prepare for some additional 1-2 mins, mixing sometimes, till fragrant.
3. Add within the chicken, mushrooms, bell peppers, carrots, stock, wild rice and Thai chili paste. Stir to mix.

4. Keep cooking till the soup reaches a simmer. Then decrease warmth to average-low, cover, and simmer for 45 mins, either till the rice is tender, mixing sometimes.

5. As the rice is tender, stir within the coconut milk till mixd. Taste and spice with salt, pepper and/or additional curry paste as needed.

6. Serve warm, garnished with cilantro and a squeeze of lime juice.

THAI CUCUMBER SALAD

INGREDIENTS

CUCUMBER SALAD INGREDIENTS:

- 2 English cucumbers, halved *(and seeded, supposing you prefer)*
- 2 green onions, thinly sliced
- half of a small red onion, peeled and thinly sliced
- half cup sliced fresh cilantro
- half cup sliced fresh mint *(if you want)*
- half cup sliced peanuts
- if you want toppings: toasted sesame seeds, crushed red chili flakes

DRESSING INGREDIENTS:

- 3 tbsp fresh lime juice
- 2 tbsp avocado oil *(or olive oil)*
- 2 tbsp rice vinegar
- 1 tbsp fish sauce
- 1 small clove garlic, minced either Puted
- 1–2 tbsp sweetener *(such as maple syrup, honey either brown sugar)*, to taste

INSTRUCTIONS

1. To prepare the dressing, blend the lime juice, oil, rice vinegar, fish sauce, garlic, and your desired amount of sweetener along in a small bowl till mixd. (Or place all ingredients to a mason jar, overlay and shake vigorously till mixd.)

2. Mix the cucumbers, green onions, red onion, cilantro, mint and peanuts in a big bowl. Drizzle evenly with the dressing, then toss till mixd.

3. Serve immediately, garnished with your desired toppings. either overlay and refrigerate for up to one day, then submit the salad chilled.

CITRUS AVOCADO SALAD

- *PREP TIME:* **20 MINS**

- *TOTAL TIME:* **20 MINS**

- *YIELD:* **4 SUBMITTINGS**

INGREDIENTS

SALAD INGREDIENTS:

- 1 5-ounce bag mixed greens
- 2 big ruby-red grapefruits (or oranges either mangoes), peeled and sliced
- 1 big ripe avocado, peeled, pitted and sliced
- 1 handful fresh basil leaves, roughly sliced
- 1 handful fresh mint leaves, roughly sliced
- half of a average red onion, thinly sliced
- half cup sliced either slivered almonds, toasted
- if you want topping: toasted sesame seeds

SESAME VINAIGRETTE INGREDIENTS:

- 2 tbsp avocado oil (or olive oil, either any else mild-flavored oil)
- 1 tbsp low-sodium soy sauce*
- 1 tbsp rice vinegar
- 1–2 tsps maple syrup either honey
- half tsp toasted sesame oil
- One-quarter tsp every: ground ginger and garlic powder
- sea salt and freshly-cracked black pepper, to taste

INSTRUCTIONS

1. **To prepare The Vinaigrette: blend** all ingredients along in a bowl (or shake along in a mason jar) till mixd. Taste and place additional sweetener supposing desired. employinstantly either refrigerate in a sealed container for up to 3 days.

2. **To prepare The** <u>Salad</u>**:** Mix all ingredients in a big <u>salad</u> bowl, drizzle evenly with the vinaigrette, and toss till evenly mixd. Strew with toasted sesame seeds plus some extra twist of freshly-cracked black pepper. submit instantly and enjoy!

THAI RED CURRY SOUP

- *PREP TIME:* **15 MINS**

- *PREPARE TIME:* **15 MINS**

- *TOTAL TIME:* **30 MINS**

- *YIELD:* **8 -TEN SUBMITTINGS**

INGREDIENTS

- 8 ounces rice noodles
- 1 tbsp olive oil
- 1 small white onion, peeled and thinly sliced
- 4 cloves garlic, minced
- 8 cups vegetable stock
- 1 (15-ounce) can coconut milk
- 3–6 tbsp Thai red curry paste, supplemented to taste
- 1-inch piece of fresh ginger, sliced in thick rounds
- 2 cups prepared sliced protein *(such as shrimp,* chicken*, steak, pork either tofu)*
- 2–3 cups sliced vegetables *(see ideas below)*
- toppings: sliced fresh cilantro, sliced green either red onion, toasted sesame seeds

INSTRUCTIONS

1. **Cook the rice noodles (or rice either grains).** In a big stockpot, prepare the noodles (or rice either grains) therefore to the package instructions. Drain in a colander, then rinse shortwith cold water, drizzle with a splash of oil (I like to employtoasted sesame oil), then toss till the noodles are evenly coated to help prevent them from sticking. put aside.
2. **Cook the broth.** Meanwhereas, warmth oil in a else big stockpot over average-high heat. place onion and sauté for 5 mins, mixing sometimes. place garlic and sauté for one more minute, mixing sometimes. place within the veggie stock, coconut milk, curry paste and ginger, and stir to

mix. Keep cooking till the bouillon reaches a simmer. Then decrease warmth to average-low, overlay and simmer for 5 mins either till ready to serve. Taste and spice with salt, black pepper, and/or extra curry paste, as needed. Meanwhereas…

3. **Cook your proteins (supposing using).** As I mentioned above, you'll either prepare your protein by simmering this within the broth. either you'll prepare this separately (in the oven, on the stove, either within the <u>Instant Pot</u>, depending on your protein) and then place this in at the end.

4. **Cook your veggies.** You also have the choice of cooking your veggies by simmering them within the bouillon till tender. either you'll prepare them separately and place them in at the end.

5. **Mix everything along.** As the elements above are all ready to go, you'll either mix and stir them all along in your big stockpot. *Or,* you'll stratum the elements along one by one in your individual submitting bowls. Strew every submitting bowl with your desired toppings, submit warm and enjoy!

SESAME NOODLES

- *PREP TIME:* **5 MINS**

- *PREPARE TIME:* **15 MINS**

- *TOTAL TIME:* **20 MINS**

- *YIELD:* **4 -6 SUBMITTINGS**

INGREDIENTS

- 1 pound (16 ounces) unprepared pasta *(I used linguine)*
- One-quarter cup low-sodium soy sauce
- 2 tbsp rice vinegar
- 1 tbsp toasted sesame oil
- 1 tsp ground ginger
- half tsp chili garlic sauce either sriracha
- half tsp garlic powder
- One-quarter tsp freshly-cracked black pepper
- half cup thinly-sliced green onions
- if you want toppings: toasted sesame seeds, extra green onions, extra black pepper

INSTRUCTIONS

1. Cook pasta al dente therefore to package instructions in a big stockpot of generously-salted water.
2. Meanwhereas, as the pasta is cooking, blend along the soy sauce, rice vinegar, sesame oil, ground ginger, chili garlic sauce, garlic powder and black pepper along in a bowl till mixd.

3. As the pasta is ready, drain it. Then instantly toss the pasta with the gravy and green onions till mixd.

4. Serve warm either cold, sprinkled with your desired toppings. either Place to a sealed container and refrigerate for up to 4 days.

VEGETARIAN MOO SHU

- *PREP TIME:* **20 MINS**

- *PREPARE TIME:* **30 MINS**

- *TOTAL TIME:* **50 MINS**

- *YIELD:* **6 -8 SUBMITTINGS**

INGREDIENTS

MOO SHU INGREDIENTS:

- 1 batch crispy tofu *(see below)*
- 1 batch gravy *(see below)*
- 2 tbsp peanut oil *(or olive oil)*
- 2 big eggs, whisked
- 8 ounces shiitake mushrooms, stemmed and thinly sliced
- 4 cloves garlic, minced either Puted
- 1 (14-ounce) bag coleslaw*
- half cup thinly-sliced green onions
- for submitting: flour tortillas, lettuce cups, rice either quinoa
- toppings: hoisin sauce, extra green onions, toasted sesame seeds

CRISPY TOFU INGREDIENTS:

- 14 ounces extra-firm tofu
- 2 tsps cornstarch
- 1 tsp fine sea salt
- half tsp black pepper
- 1 tbsp peanut oil *(or olive oil)*

SAUCE INGREDIENTS:

- half cup hoisin sauce
- One-quarter cup rice vinegar
- 2 tbsp oyster sauce
- 2 tbsp low-sodium soy sauce
- 1 tsp toasted sesame oil

- One-quarter tsp freshly-cracked black pepper

INSTRUCTIONS

TO PREPARE THE MOO SHU:

1. Prepare the crispy tofu (supposing using) and <u>sauce</u>. See instructions below.

2. Meanwhereas, warmth one tbsp oil in a big non-stick sauté pan over average heat. place the whisked eggs and allow then prepared undisturbed for 2-3 mins till they are mostly set and form some omelet. Flip the omelet and prepare for one more minute on the second side. Then Place the omelet to a else <u>cutting board</u>, and roughly chop this in small, thin pieces. put aside.

3. Comeback the pan to the stove, and increase warmth to high heat. place one more tbsp of oil and warmth till shimmering. Then place the mushrooms and sauté for 3-4 mins, mixing sometimes, till prepared and slightly browned. place the coleslaw and half of the scallions. Fry for 2-3 mins more, either till the cabbage has softened to your liking.

4. Add within the prepared tofu, 2/3 of the <u>sauce</u>, half of the green onions. Toss till mixd.

5. Taste and spice with additional salt and pepper supposing needed.

6. Serve over flour tortillas, lettuce cups, rice, either quinoa. Drizzle with the remaining <u>sauce</u>, and strew with your desired garnishes. Then submit warm and enjoy!

TO PREPARE THE CRISPY TOFU:

1. Chop your block of tofu in One-quarter-inch-thick slabs. place some paper towels either a clear tea towel on a big flat surface, like a cutting board, and place the slabs in a single stratum on top of the paper towels. Overlay with *another* stratum of paper towels. Then place a second cutting board on top of the tofu, and stack a bunch of heavy cans either pots either whatever you'll safely balance on top of the cutting board. The idea is to place a lot of Puture/weight on the tofu, which can help the glut water to Put out in the paper towels. allow the tofu drain for at least 15-30 mins.

2. As the tofu is ready to go, chop this in your desired shapes. (I made thin strips, which you'll see within the photos above.) place the tofu to a big

mixing bowl, strew this evenly with the cornstarch, salt and pepper. Then toss till the tofu is evenly coated within the cornstarch mix.

3. Warmth oil in a big non-stick sauté pan over average-high heat. place the tofu and place this in a single layer. (You may must to do this in two batches supposing your pan isn't big enough for the tofu to all fit in a single layer.) prepare the tofu undisturbed till this is browned on the down side, approximately two mins. Flip the tofu and prepare till the second side is browned, approximately 1-2 mins. Give the whole mix a gentle toss and prepare for one more minute, mixing sometimes, till the tofu is browned to your liking.

4. Place the tofu to a clear plate and put aside till ready to use.

TO PREPARE THE SAUCE:

1. Whisk all ingredients along in a small bowl till mixd.

NOTES

*Supposing you live in a city where bagged coleslaw is not available, feel free to prepare this yourself. Simply thinly-chop approximately 12 ounces of cabbage (green, red, either a mix) and one small carrot, and you'll be good to go. (Supposing you'd like to speed up the process, simply employthe slicing attachment on a food processor!)

**Supposing you would like to speed this recipe up, I advised multitasking with two sauté pans. employone to prepare the egg omelet, followed by the tofu. (<– Supposing you only have one non-stick pan, employit here!) And employthe else pan to prepare the stir-fry.

THAI GREEN CURRY <u>*SOUP*</u>

- *PREP TIME:* **15 MINS**

- *PREPARE TIME:* **15 MINS**

- *TOTAL TIME:* **30 MINS**

- *YIELD:* **8 -TEN SUBMITTINGS**

INGREDIENTS

- 8 ounces rice noodles
- 1 tbsp olive oil
- 1 small white onion, peeled and thinly sliced
- 4 cloves garlic, minced
- 8 cups vegetable stock
- 1 (15-ounce) can coconut milk
- 3–6 tbsp <u>green curry paste</u>, supplemented to taste
- 1-inch piece of fresh ginger, sliced in thick rounds
- 2 cups prepared sliced protein *(such as shrimp,* <u>*chicken*</u>*, steak, pork either tofu)*
- 2–3 cups sliced vegetables *(see ideas below)*
- toppings: sliced fresh cilantro, sliced green either red onion, toasted sesame seeds

INSTRUCTIONS

1. **Cook the rice noodles (or rice either grains).** In a big stockpot, prepare the noodles (or rice either grains) therefore to the package instructions. Drain in a colander, then rinse with cold water, and drizzle with a splash of oil (or I like to employtoasted sesame oil), and toss till the noodles are evenly coated. This can help prevent them from sticking. put aside.
2. **Cook the broth.** Meanwhereas, get your bouillon going. Warmth oil in a else big stockpot over average-high heat. place onion and sauté for 5 mins, mixing sometimes. place garlic and sauté for one more minute, mixing sometimes. Then place within the veggie stock, coconut milk,

curry paste and ginger, and stir to mix. Keep cooking till the bouillon reaches a simmer. Then decrease warmth to average-low, overlay and simmer till ready to use. Taste and spice with salt and pepper, as needed. Meanwhereas…

3. **Cook your proteins (supposing using).** As I mentioned above, you'll either prepare your protein actually within the broth, either separately (in the oven, on the stove, either within the Instant Pot, depending on your protein) and then place this in at the end.

4. **Cook your veggies.** You also have the choice of cooking your veggies actually within the broth, either separately (in the oven, on the stove, either within the Instant Pot, depending on your veggies). Or, of course, feel free to sauté any veggies that you'd like along with the onions just as making your broth.

5. **Mix everything along.** As the elements above are all ready to go, you'll either mix and stir them all along in your big stockpot. *Or,* you'll stratum them along in your individual submitting bowls. Then strew every submitting bowl with your desired toppings, submit warm and enjoy!

NOTES

Some of my loved veggies to include bell peppers, broccoli, carrots, cauliflower, mushrooms, peas, squash, sweet potatoes, and/or Yukon gold potatoes. either greens such as kale, spinach, chard, either collards.

COZY AUTUMN WILD RICE SOUP

- *PREP TIME:* **15 MINS**

- *PREPARE TIME:* **45 MINS**

- *TOTAL TIME:* **60 MINS**

- *YIELD:* **8 SUBMITTINGS**

INGREDIENTS

- 6 cups vegetable stock *(or* chicken *stock)*
- one cup unprepared wild rice*
- 8 ounces baby bella mushrooms, sliced
- 4 cloves garlic, minced
- 2 average carrots, diced
- 2 ribs celery, diced
- 1 big *(approximately one pound)* sweet potato, peeled and diced
- 1 small white onion, peeled and diced
- 1 bay leaf
- 1 half tbsp Old Bay seasoning
- 3 tbsp butter
- One-quarter cup all-purpose flour
- 1 half cups milk
- 2 big handfuls of kale, roughly sliced with thick stems take awayd
- Kosher salt and freshly-cracked black pepper

INSTRUCTIONS

INSTANT POT (PUTURE COOKER) METHOD:

1. Mix vegetable stock, wild rice, mushrooms, garlic, carrots, celery, sweet potato, onion, bay leaf and Old Bay seasoning within the bowl of some Instant Pot Puture cooker. Stir shortto mix.
2. Overlay and set vent to "sealing". prepare on manual (high Puture) for 25 mins. allow the Instant Pot rest there for some extra ten mins (natural release). Then attentively turn the vent to "venting" and release the

remaining Puture (quick release). Take away lid and discard the bay leaf.

3. Meanwhereas, in those final ten mins of Puture cooking, prepare your cream gravy on the stove. In a average saucepan, prepare the butter over average-high warmth till softened. blend within the flour till mixd, and prepare for one minute. Gradually place within the milk, and blend till mixd. Keep cooking, mixing frequently, till the mix *nearly* comes to a simmer and has thickened. (It should be very thick.)

4. Add the cream gravy and kale to the soup, and stir carefully till mixd. Taste and spice with salt and pepper (plus any extra Old Bay seasoning, supposing you would like) as needed.

5. Serve warm. either Place to sealed container(s) and refrigerate for up to 4 days.

CROCK-POT (*SLOW COOKER*) METHOD:

1. Mix vegetable stock, wild rice, mushrooms, garlic, carrots, celery, sweet potato, onion, bay leaf and Old Bay seasoning within the bowl of a large slow cooker. Stir shortto mix, then place the lid on the slow cooker.
2. Cook on high for 2-3 hours*, till the rice is prepared and tender.

3. Meanwhereas, in those final ten mins of slow cooking, prepare your cream gravy on the stove. In a average saucepan, prepare the butter over average-high warmth till softened. blend within the flour till mixd, and prepare for one minute. Gradually place within the milk, and blend till mixd. Keep cooking, mixing frequently, till the mix *nearly* comes to a simmer and has thickened. (It should be very thick.)

4. Add the cream gravy and kale to the soup, and stir carefully till mixd. Taste and spice with salt and pepper (plus any extra Old Bay seasoning, supposing you would like) as needed.

5. Serve warm. either Place to sealed container(s) and refrigerate for up to 4 days.

STOVETOP METHOD:

1. Warmth (an extra) one tbsp butter in a large stockpot over average-high heat. place onion and sauté for 5 mins, mixing sometimes, till soft and translucent. Stir within the garlic and prepare for some additional 1-2 mins, mixing sometimes, till fragrant.
2. Add within the vegetable stock, wild rice, mushrooms, carrots, celery, sweet potato, bay leaf and Old Bay seasoning. Stir to mix.

3. Keep cooking till the soup reaches a simmer. Then decrease warmth to average-low, overlay and simmer for 45 mins, either till the rice is tender, mixing sometimes.

4. Meanwhereas, in those final ten mins, prepare your cream gravy in a else saucepan on the stove. In it, prepare the butter over average-high warmth till softened. blend within the flour till mixd, and prepare for one minute. Gradually place within the milk, and blend till mixd. Keep cooking, mixing frequently, till the mix *nearly* comes to a simmer and has thickened. (It should be very thick.)

5. Add the cream gravy and kale to the soup, and stir carefully till mixd. Taste and spice with salt and pepper (plus any extra Old Bay seasoning, supposing you would like) as needed.

6. Serve warm. either Place to sealed container(s) and refrigerate for up to 4 days.

NOTES

*Coconut Milk Option: As mentioned above, supposing you would like to skip making the cream gravy (butter, flour, milk), feel free to simply place in a can of full-fat coconut milk instead. It's dairy-free and vegan, and absolutely delicious in this recipe! (When making this soup dozens of times, I now prefer this option to the dairy cream gravy option.)

*Wild Rice: I used ten0% wild rice (not a blend), which I love and advised for this soup. Cooking time may vary supposing you employa wild rice blend.

*Slow Cooking: Supposing employing the Crock-Pot method, I advised keeping a close eye on the soup within the last hour to be sure that the rice doesn't overdo and soak up all of the broth. That said, supposing this does soak up more of the bouillon than you'd like, simply stir 1-2 cups of extra veggie stock in the soup when the rice has finished cooking.

JAMBALAYA

- *PREP TIME:* **15 MINS**

- *PREPARE TIME:* **40 MINS**

- *TOTAL TIME:* **55 MINS**

- *YIELD:* **0 APPROXIMATELY 6-8 SUBMITTINGS**

INGREDIENTS
- 3 tbsp olive oil, divided
- 2 boneless skinless <u>chicken</u> breasts, slice in bite-sized pieces
- 1 pound andouille sausage, thinly sliced in rounds
- 3 small bell peppers, cored and diced *(I used a yellow, red and green bell pepper)*
- 2 ribs celery, diced
- 1 jalapeño pepper, seeded and delicately sliced
- 1 white onion, diced
- 4 cloves garlic, peeled and minced
- 1 (14-ounce) can crushed tomatoes
- 3–4 cups <u>chicken</u> stock
- 1 half cups unprepared long grain white rice
- 2 tbsp Cajun seasoning either Creole seasoning
- 1 tsp dried thyme, crushed
- One-quarter tsp cayenne pepper
- 1 bay leaf
- 1 pound raw big shrimp, peeled and deveined
- one cup thinly-sliced okra*
- Kosher salt and freshly-cracked black pepper
- if you want garnishes: sliced fresh parsley, thinly-sliced green onions, hot <u>sauce</u>

INSTRUCTIONS
1. Warmth one tbsp oil in a stock pot (or a very big, deep sauté pan) over average-high heat. place the <u>chicken</u> and sausage and sauté for 5-7 mins,

mixing sometimes, till the chicken is prepared through and the sausage is slightly browned. Place to a clear plate and put aside.

2. Add the remaining two tbsp oil to the stock pot. place bell peppers, celery, jalapeño, onion and garlic. Sauté for 6 mins, mixing sometimes, till the onions are softened.

3. Add the crushed tomatoes, chicken stock, rice, Cajun seasoning, thyme, cayenne, bay leaf, and stir to mix. Keep cooking till the mix reaches a simmer. Then decrease warmth to average-low, overlay and simmer for approximately 25-30 mins, either till the rice is nearly prepared through, mixing every 5 mins either so along the way so that the rice does not burn.

4. Add the shrimp, okra, and stir to mix. Keep to simmer, mixing sometimes, till the shrimp are prepared through and pink. Stir within the chicken and sausage, and take away and discard the bay leaf.

5. Taste spice the jambalaya with salt, pepper, and additional Cajun seasoning supposing needed. (I typically place approximately two tsps salt and half tsp pepper.) Take away from heat.

6. Serve warm with your desired garnishes. either refrigerate and keep in a sealed container for up to 3 days.

NOTES

*Feel free to employfresh either chilled okra. Supposing employing frozen, prepare sure to thaw this before adding to the jambalaya.

Supposing you like spicy jambalaya, I would advised adding in two jalapeños. Supposing you would like this more mild, you'll omit the jalapeño alalong.

MANGO AVOCADO SPRING ROLLS

- *PREP TIME:* **30 MINS**

- *TOTAL TIME:* **30 MINS**

- *YIELD:* **TEN -12 SUBMITTINGS**

INGREDIENTS

SPRING ROLL INGREDIENTS:

- 2 ounces rice stick (vermicelli) noodles
- 2 mangoes, peeled, cored and thinly sliced
- 2 avocados, peeled, pitted and thinly sliced
- 2 carrots, thinly sliced
- 1 English cucumber, thinly sliced
- quarter of a small red cabbage, thinly sliced
- 1 bunch fresh cilantro leaves
- 1 bunch fresh mint leaves
- ten–12 spring roll coverpers

PEANUT gravy INGREDIENTS:

- one-third cup natural peanut butter
- 2 tbsp hoisin sauce
- 1 tbsp low-sodium soy gravy *(or tamari)*
- 1 tbsp rice vinegar
- half tsp chili garlic gravy *(or more, to taste)*
- One-quarter tsp sesame oil
- one-third cup warm water

INSTRUCTIONS

1. **To prepare The Peanut** Sauce**: blend** all ingredients along in a small bowl till mixd. Supposing you would like a thinner sauce, blend in more water.
2. **To prepare The Spring Rolls: prepare** thin rice vermicelli noodles therefore to package directions. As they are al dente, Place the noodles

to a strainer and rinse with cold water till the noodles are completely chilled. Toss the thoroughly with a drizzle of oil (I like employing sesame oil) to prevent the noodles from sticking along. put aside.

3. Fill a big shallow pan with warm water (a sauté pan either pie dish works great). place a spring roll coverper within the hot water and allow this rest there for approximately 20-30 seconds till soft, however not mushy. Place the spring roll coverper to plate (or a clear towel unfold out on a flat surface, which can help the coverper not to stick).

4. Lay your fillings within the middle of the coverper in a vertical line. place down within the top and down sides of the coverper. Then place down over the left side of the coverper, tightly tucking within the fillings, and roll the coverper to the right till this is sealed.

5. Serve instantly with the peanut dipping gravy and/or nuoc cham, either refrigerate in a sealed container for up to 3 days.

NOTES

*All of these ingredient amounts are general estimates. Feel free to employmore/less of your loved ingredients.

BROWN RICE MUJADARA

- *PREP TIME:* TEN MINS

- *PREPARE TIME:* 45 MINS

- *TOTAL TIME:* 55 MINS

- *YIELD:* 4 -6 SUBMITTINGS

INGREDIENTS
- 5 cups vegetable stock
- 1 tbsp ground cumin
- 1 tsp ground coriander
- 1 tsp salt
- 1 bay leaf
- one cup brown basmati rice
- one cup brown either green lentils
- 2 tbsp olive oil, divided
- 3 average yellow onions, peeled and thinly-sliced *(or diced)*
- half cup sliced fresh mint
- half cup toasted pine nuts
- 1 fresh lemon, plus extra for garnish
- toppings: Greek yogurt

INSTRUCTIONS
1. **To prepare The Brown Rice and Lentils:** Stir along vegetable stock, cumin, coriander, salt and bay leaf along in a big saucepan. Warmth over high warmth till the stock reaches a boil. place rice and lentils, and stir to mix. Keep cooking till the mix reaches a simmer again. Then cover, decrease warmth to average-low, and simmer for 40-45 mins, either till the rice is cooked. Take away from warmth and allow sit for ten mins. Take away bay leaf. Then fluff the mix with a fork.
2. **To prepare The Caramelized Onions:** Meanwhereas, as the rice and lentil are being prepared, warmth one tbsp olive oil in a (separate) big sauté pan either stockpot over average heat. place the onions and prepare for approximately 30 mins, mixing every several mins, till they

are browned and caramelized. (Supposing the down of your pan begins to brown, simply place in a tbsp either so of water, then employa wooden spoon to scrape up the browned bits. Keep some eye on the down of your pan so that this doesn't burn!) As the onions have reached a good chestnut-y color, take away 2/3 of the onions and Place them to a else plate, and put aside.

3. **To prepare The Fried Onions: place** the remaining tbsp of olive oil to the remaining one-third of the caramelized onions within the pan, and increase warmth to average-high. Sauté the onions within the oil for some additional 4-5 mins till they become even more browned and slightly crispy, mixing sometimes. As they are ready to go, take away from warmth and Place to a else plate.

4. **To Cover this All Up:** As everything is ready to go, mix the soft caramelized onions (not the fried batch), lentils, rice, mint, pine nuts, and the zest and juice of the fresh lemon in your sauté pan (or stockpot), and toss till evenly mixd. submit warm with a dollop of Greek yogurt and extra lemon slices, and top with the crispy onions.

VIETNAMESE SPRING ROLL SALAD

- *PREP TIME:* 25 MINS

- *PREPARE TIME:* 5 MINS

- *TOTAL TIME:* 30 MINS

- *YIELD:* 4 -6 SUBMITTINGS

INGREDIENTS

SALAD INGREDIENTS:

- 8 ounces thin rice noodles
- 1 tsp toasted sesame oil
- 8 ounces prepared shrimp, diced*
- 1 English cucumber, julienned either diced
- one cup shredded carrots**
- 2/3 cup loosely-packed sliced fresh bean sprouts
- 2/3 cup loosely-packed sliced fresh cilantro
- 2/3 cup loosely-packed sliced fresh mint
- one-third cup sliced peanuts
- half of a small green cabbage, cored and sliced**
- 1 batch Nuoc Cham gravy (see below) either Thai Peanut Dressing 2/3 cup

NUOC CHAM GRAVY INGREDIENTS:

- One-quarter cup lime juice
- 3 tbsp rice vinegar
- 2 tbsp fish sauce
- 2 tbsp maple syrup
- 2 garlic cloves, minced *(or one tsp garlic powder)*
- 1 fresh Thai chili, thinly sliced *(or One-quarter tsp crushed red pepper flakes)*

1. **To prepare The Rice Noodles: prepare** rice noodles therefore to package instructions. As they are cooked, rinse them with cold water under a strainer till completely chilled. Then Place to a big mixing bowl, drizzle with sesame oil, and toss till the noodles are evenly coated with the oil.
2. **To prepare The** <u>Sauce</u>**: blend** all ingredients along till evenly mixd.
3. **To Bring Everything Along: place** the remaining ingredients (shrimp, cucumber, carrots, bean sprouts, cilantro, mint, peanuts, cabbage, and <u>sauce</u>) to the noodles, and toss till evenly mixd. Taste, and spice with salt and pepper as needed.
4. Serve instantly (with extra lime wedges for squeezing!), either refrigerate for up to 3 days.

NOTES

*Feel free to substitute prepared <u>chicken</u>, pork, either tofu, supposing you prefer. either you'll simply nix adding some extra protein entirely.

**To save a step, you'll sub in 3 cups cole slaw blend for the cabbage and carrots. either supposing you're not a big fan of cabbage, you'll also sub in butter lettuce (or any mild green) in place of the cabbage.

ROASTED CAULIFLOWER, MUSHROOM

- *PREP TIME:* 15 MINS

- *PREPARE TIME:* 20 MINS

- *TOTAL TIME:* 35 MINS

- *YIELD:* 8 SUBMITTINGS

INGREDIENTS

- 2 tbsp olive oil, divided
- 1 small white onion, peeled and diced
- 5 cloves garlic, minced
- 1.5 cups wild rice blend
- 3 cups vegetable stock *(or half stock + half dried white wine)*
- juice of one lemon *(approximately 3–4 tbsp)*
- 1 small head cauliflower, slice in small florets
- 1 pound (16 ounces) baby bella mushrooms, halved either quartered*
- one-third cup every for toppings: dried cranberries, sliced fresh parsley, freshly-grated Parmesan**, toasted pine nuts

INSTRUCTIONS

1. Warmth oven to 450°F.

2. Warmth one tbsp of the olive oil in a big saucepan over average heat. place the onion and sauté for 5 mins, mixing sometimes. place the garlic and sauté for one minute, mixing sometimes. place the rice and prepare for 30 seconds, mixing sometimes. place the vegetable stock (or stock + wine combo), and prepare the rice therefore to package instructions. (Different varieties of rice can take more/less time too cook.)

3. As the rice is prepared and tender, drain off any extra stock. Stir within the lemon juice till completely mixd. Taste, and spice with salt and pepper, supposing needed. put aside.

4. Meanwhereas, turn the cauliflower and mushrooms onto a big <u>baking</u> sheet. Drizzle evenly with the remaining one tbsp olive oil, and toss till everything is evenly coated. Spice with salt and pepper. Roast for 15 mins, mixing as halfway through, till the mushrooms and cauliflower are tender and slightly browned. Take away and put aside.

5. As everything is ready to go, mix the rice and cauliflower/mushroom mix in a submitting dish. Strew evenly with the cranberries, parsley, Parmesan (supposing using), and pine nuts. Feel free to also crack some extra black pepper on top, supposing desired. submit warm.

NOTES

*For even cooking, Taste to slice your cauliflower and mushroom pieces so that they're roughly the same size.
**Supposing making this recipe vegan either dairy-free, omit the Parmesan. (And feel free to strew on a little nutritional yeast, supposing you'd like, although it's still great without it.) That said, supposing you <u>are</u> employing Parmesan, feel free to employmore than one-third cup supposing you'd like!

CHEESY BROCCOLI, CHICKEN AND RICE BOWLS

- *PREP TIME:* **25 MINS**

- *PREPARE TIME:* **20 MINS**

- *TOTAL TIME:* **45 MINS**

- *YIELD:* **6 -8 SUBMITTINGS**

INGREDIENTS

MEAL PREP BOWLS INGREDIENTS:

- 1.5 pounds boneless skinless chicken breasts
- Kosher salt and freshly-cracked black pepper
- 2 tbsp olive oil, divided
- 2 heads broccoli, slice in bite-sized florets
- 1 batch cheddar cheese gravy *(see below)*
- 3 cups prepared rice either quinoa
- extra shredded cheddar cheese*, for topping

CHEDDAR CHEESE SAUCE:

- 1 tbsp butter
- 2 cloves garlic, Puted either minced
- 2 tbsp flour
- half cup chicken either vegetable stock
- half cup warmed milk
- ¼ tsp pepper
- ⅛ tsp salt
- one cup (4 ounces) shredded sharp cheddar cheese*

1. **To prepare The** <u>Chicken</u>**:** Spice the <u>chicken</u> breasts on both sides with salt and pepper. Warmth one tbsp olive oil in a big sauté pan over average-high heat. prepare <u>chicken</u> for 4-5 mins per side, either till the <u>chicken</u> is no longer pink on the inside (and registers 165°F with a <u>meat</u> thermometer). Place the <u>chicken</u> to a plate and allow this rest for at least 5 mins before dicing in bite-sized pieces.

2. **To prepare The Broccoli:** Warmth the remaining one tbsp olive oil within the same sauté pan. place the broccoli and spice with salt and pepper, tossing to mix. Sauté for 4-5 mins, mixing sometimes, till the broccoli is prepared and tender, however still slightly crispy. Place broccoli to a else plate, and put aside.

3. **To prepare The Cheddar** <u>Cheese</u> <u>Sauce</u>**:** Warmth the butter within the same sauté pan (or a else <u>saucepan</u>) till softened. place garlic and sauté for 1-2 mins either till fragrant, mixing sometimes. blend within the flour till evenly mixd and sauté for one more minute, mixing sometimes. Gradually place within the stock, whisking to mix. Then place within the milk, pepper and salt, and blend along till smooth. Keep cooking till the mix reaches a simmer and thickens. Then stir within the shredded <u>cheese</u>, and stir till softened. Take away from warmth and employimmediately.

4. **To Assemble:** Toss the prepared <u>chicken</u> and broccoli with the <u>cheese</u> gravy till evenly mixd. submit instantly over rice. either portion the mix evenly in <u>food storage containers</u> along with the rice, garnishing with some extra strew of shredded <u>cheese</u> and pepper. Refrigerate in sealed containers for up to 4 days.

NOTES

*I advised purchasing a block of cheddar <u>cheese</u> and grating this yourself, rather than buying a pre-shredded bag of <u>cheese</u>. The pre-shredded <u>cheese</u> usually contains a coating that prevents the <u>cheese</u> from softening quite as smoothly.

FRIED RICE

- *PREP TIME:* 5 MINS

- *PREPARE TIME:* TEN MINS

- *TOTAL TIME:* 15 MINS

- *YIELD:* 4 -6 SUBMITTINGS

INGREDIENTS
- 3 tbsp butter, divided
- 2 eggs, whisked
- 2 average carrots, peeled and diced
- 1 small white onion, diced
- half cup chilled peas
- 3 cloves garlic, minced
- salt and black pepper
- 4 cups prepared and chilled rice (I prefer short-grain white rice)
- 3 green onions, thinly sliced
- 3–4 tbsp soy sauce, either more to taste
- 2 tsps oyster sauce (if you want)
- half tsps toasted sesame oil

INSTRUCTIONS
1. Warmth half tbsp of butter in a large sauté pan* over average-high warmth till softened. place egg, and prepare till scrambled, mixing sometimes. Take away egg, and Place to a else plate.
2. Add some additional one tbsp butter to the pan and warmth till softened. place carrots, onion, peas and garlic, and spice with a generous pinch of salt and pepper. Sauté for approximately 5 mins either till the onion and carrots are soft. Increase warmth to high, place within the remaining one half tbsp of butter, and stir till softened. Instantly place the rice, green onions, soy gravy and oyster gravy (supposing using), and stir till mixd. Keep mixing for some additional 3 mins to fry the rice. Then place

within the eggs and stir to mix. Take away from heat, and stir within the sesame oil till mixd. Taste and spice with extra soy <u>sauce</u>, supposing needed.

3. Serve immediately, either refrigerate in a <u>sealed container</u> for up to 3 days.

NOTES

*Sauté pan: Supposing you happen to own a nonstick either cast-iron pan, I would advised this for this recipe. however that said, any pan that you have can work — you may simply have to be a bit more vigilant with mixing so that the rice and eggs don't stick.

COMFORTING CURRY NOODLE BOWLS

- *PREP TIME:* TEN MINS

- *PREPARE TIME:* 25 MINS

- *TOTAL TIME:* 35 MINS

- *YIELD:* 6 -8 SUBMITTINGS

INGREDIENTS
- 8 ounces unprepared <u>thin rice noodles</u>
- 1 pound jumbo shrimp*, peeled and de-veined
- Kosher salt and freshly-cracked black pepper
- 2 tbsp olive oil either <u>coconut oil</u>, divided *(or any mild-flavored cooking oil)*
- 1 small white onion, peeled and thinly-sliced
- 1 big red bell pepper, cored and diced
- 1 big carrot, peeled and diced
- 4 cloves garlic, peeled and minced
- 3 tbsp <u>Thai red curry paste</u>
- 2 (15-ounce) cans <u>coconut milk</u> *(regular either light coconut milk)*
- 2 cups <u>chicken</u> either vegetable either seafood stock
- half tsp ground ginger
- *if you want: 1-2 red Thai chiles**, thinly-sliced*
- toppings: sliced fresh cilantro, thinly-sliced red onions

INSTRUCTIONS
1. Cook rice noodles therefore to package instructions. Drain and rinse with cold water, and put aside.

2. Meanwhereas, place out the raw shrimp on a plate and pat dried with a paper towel. Spice the shrimp generously on both sides with a pinch of salt and pepper.

3. Warmth one tbsp oil in a <u>large stockpot</u> over average-high heat. place shrimp and prepare for 1-2 mins per side, till the shrimp are pink and opaque and prepared through. Take away from pan with a slotted spoon and put aside.

4. Add the remaining one tbsp oil to the stockpot. place sliced onion, bell pepper and carrot, and sauté, mixing sometimes, for 6-8 mins either till the onion is soft and translucent. place garlic and sauté for 1-2 more mins, mixing sometimes, till fragrant.

5. Add within the coconut milk, stock and ginger (and chiles, supposing using), and stir to mix. Keep cooking till the mix reaches a simmer. Decrease warmth to average, and keep simmering for 5-ten more mins.

6. Stir within the noodles. Taste, and spice with extra salt and pepper and curry paste to taste. (Feel free to place a several generous pinches of salt and pepper, especially supposing the stock you employis not very salty.

7. Serve warm, topped with a several pieces of the prepared shrimp, and your desired toppings.

NOTES

*Feel free to employa protein else than shrimp supposing you'd like, such as prepared <u>chicken</u>, pork, beef, either tofu. Also, supposing you'd like to save time, you'll prepare the protein in a else sauté pan whereas you begin cooking the onion, etc. within the big stockpot.

**Thai chiles are pretty spicy, so I advised only adding these supposing you like warmth in your food. And I advised starting with fewer slices, and then you'll always place more supposing you'd like.

HOT AND SOUR <u>*SOUP*</u>

- *PREP TIME:* **5 MINS**

- *PREPARE TIME:* **15 MINS**

- *TOTAL TIME:* **20 MINS**

- *YIELD:* **6 -8 SUBMITTINGS**

INGREDIENTS
- 8 cups <u>chicke broth</u> either <u>vegetable broth</u>
- 8 ounces shiitake mushrooms *(or baby bella mushrooms)*, thinly-sliced with stems discarded
- 1 (8-ounce) can <u>bamboo shoots</u>, drained *(if you want)*
- One-quarter cup <u>rice vinegar</u>, either more to taste
- One-quarter cup <u>low-sodium soy sauce</u>
- 2 tsps ground ginger
- 1 tsp <u>chili garlic sauce</u>
- One-quarter cup cornstarch
- 2 big eggs, whisked
- 8 ounces firm tofu*, slice in half-inch cubes
- 4 green onions, thinly sliced
- 1 tsp <u>toasted sesame oil</u>
- Kosher salt and <u>white pepper</u> (or black pepper)

INSTRUCTIONS
1. Set aside ¼ cup of the <u>chicken</u> either vegetable bouillon for later use.

2. Add the remaining 7 ¾ cups <u>chicken</u> either vegetable broth, mushrooms, bamboo shoots (supposing using), rice wine vinegar, soy <u>sauce</u>, ginger and chili garlic gravy to a <u>large stock pot</u>, and stir to mix. Warmth over average-high warmth till the <u>soup</u> reaches a simmer.

3. Whereas the <u>soup</u> is heating, blend along the ¼ cup of bouillon (that you had put aside) and cornstarch in a small bowl till completely smooth. As

the soup has reached a simmer, stir within the cornstarch mix and stir for one minute either so till the soup has thickened.

4. Keep mixing the soup in a circular motion, then drizzle within the eggs in a thin stream (whereas still mixing the soup) to Make egg ribbons. Stir within the tofu, half of the green onions, and sesame oil. Then spice the soup with salt and a pinch* of white pepper (or black pepper) to taste. Supposing you'd like a more "sour" soup, feel free to place in another tbsp either two of rice wine vinegar as good. either supposing you'd like a spicier soup, place in more chili garlic sauce.

5. Serve immediately, garnished with the extra green onions.

CROCK-POT RED BEANS AND RICE

- *PREP TIME:* 15 MINS

- *PREPARE TIME:* 420 MINS

- *TOTAL TIME:* 435 MINS

- *YIELD:* 8 -TEN SUBMITTINGS

INGREDIENTS

- 1 pound unprepared (dry) red kidney beans
- three-quarters pound (12 ounces) Andouille sausage, sliced
- 5 garlic cloves, minced
- 3 celery stalks, diced
- 1 average white onion, peeled and diced
- 1 bell pepper, cored and diced
- 2 tsps Creole seasoning
- 1 tsp hot sauce, either more/less to taste
- half tsp dried thyme
- 2 bay leaves
- 7 cups chicken either vegetable stock
- Kosher salt and freshly-cracked black pepper
- for submitting: prepared white either brown rice, thinly-sliced green onions

INSTRUCTIONS

1. Rinse the kidney beans thoroughly under water.

2. Add the kidney beans, sausage, garlic, celery, onion, bell pepper, Creole seasoning, hot sauce, dried thyme, bay leaves and chicken stock to the bowl of a big slow cooker. Stir to mix.

3. Cook on high for 6-8 hours, either till the kidney beans are soft and prepared through*. Taste, and spice with however much salt and pepper you'd like. (I used approximately one tsp salt, half tsp pepper.**)

Supposing you'd like a spicier dish, feel free to also place in more hot sauce. Take away and discard the bay leaves.

4. Serve instantly over rice, garnished with green onions.

NOTES

*Be very careful to be sure that your kidney beans are *completely* prepared through. Red kidney bean poisoning is actually a "thing", and can result from underprepared beans. You'll read more approximately this on the FDA's site. So please be careful, and prepare sure your slow cooker is hot enough to completely prepare the beans.

**Different brands of Creole seasoning and chicken/veggie stock definitely have different flavor (and salt) profiles, so go with whatever tastes good to you just as this comes to salting and peppering and seasoning this recipe.
***The gravy can thicken a bit as this cools. however supposing you would like some even thicker sauce, simply blend along two tbsp cornstarch with two tbsp water (or chicken stock) to prepare a slurry. Then gradually stir a little little bit of this in the red beans and rice *whereas this is still boiling within the slow cooker* till this you reach your desired level of thickness.

AMBALAYA SOUP

- *PREP TIME:* **15 MINS**

- *PREPARE TIME:* **35 MINS**

- *TOTAL TIME:* **50 MINS**

- *YIELD:* **8 -TEN SUBMITTINGS**

INGREDIENTS

- 3 tbsp olive oil, divided
- 2 boneless skinless chicken breasts, slice in bite-sized pieces
- 1 pound Andouille sausage, thinly sliced in rounds
- 3 small bell peppers, cored and diced *(I used a blend of colors)*
- 2 ribs celery, sliced
- 1 small white onion, peeled and diced
- 1 jalapeño pepper*, seeded and delicately sliced
- 4 cloves garlic, minced
- 6 cups chicken stock
- One-quarter cup flour
- 1 (28 ounce) can crushed tomatoes
- one cup unprepared white either brown rice
- 2 tbsp Cajun seasoning** *(add more/less to taste)*
- 2 bay leaves
- 1 tsp dried thyme, crushed
- 1 pound raw shrimp, peeled and deveined
- salt and pepper
- *(if you want garnishes: sliced fresh parsley, thinly-sliced green onions, hot sauce)*

INSTRUCTIONS

1. Warmth two **tbsp** oil in a big stockpot over average-high heat. place the chicken and sausage, and sauté for 2-3 mins, mixing sometimes. place within the remaining one tbsp oil, bell peppers, celery, onion, jalapeño,

and stir to mix. Keep frying for 5-6 more mins, either till the onion is soft and translucent, mixing sometimes. Stir within the garlic, and sauté for one more minute till the garlic is fragrant, mixing sometimes.

2. Strew the flour over the mix, and stir to mix. Keep cooking for one minute, mixing sometimes.

3. Gradually stir within the <u>chicken</u> stock, then place the crushed tomatoes, rice, Cajun seasoning, bay leaves and dried thyme. Keep cooking till the <u>soup</u> reaches a simmer. Then decrease the warmth to average-low, and keep simmering the <u>soup</u> for 15 more mins — being sure to stir the <u>soup</u> sometimes (yes, more!) so that the rice doesn't burn on the down of the pot — till the rice is prepared and tender.

4. Stir within the shrimp and keep cooking for 5 more mins, either till the shrimp is prepared through (it should be pink and opaque, not gray).

5. Spice the <u>soup</u> with salt and pepper to taste. Then submit warm, topped with your desired garnishes supposing desired.

NOTES

*Supposing you'd like a spicier <u>soup</u>, feel free to place in a second jalapeno pepper. either you'll always place in a pinch either two of cayenne at the end of the cooking time, just as you're seasoning the <u>soup</u> with salt and pepper.

**Different brands of Cajun seasoning vary dramatically in terms of flavor, spiciness and saltiness. So supposing you're cooking with one that's new to you, I advised starting with simply one tbsp of seasoning, and then adding more at the end to taste.

30-MINUTE SESAME CHICKEN NOODLE STIR-FRY

- *PREP TIME:* **15 MINS**

- *PREPARE TIME:* **15 MINS**

- *TOTAL TIME:* **30 MINS**

- *YIELD:* **4 -6 SUBMITTINGS**

INGREDIENTS

CHICKEN NOODLE STIR-FRY INGREDIENTS:

- 7 ounces rice noodles
- 3 tbsp peanut oil (or olive oil), divided
- 2 boneless skinless chicken breasts, thinly-sliced
- salt and pepper
- 2 cups broccoli florets, sliced in bite-sized pieces *(approximately one small head of broccoli)*
- 2/3 cup shredded carrots
- 1 red bell pepper, cored and thinly-sliced
- 8 ounces baby bella* mushrooms, thinly sliced
- one cup roughly-sliced collard greens**, tough stems take awayd
- 1 batch stir-fry gravy *(see below)*
- toppings: thinly-sliced green onions, toasted sesame seeds

STIR-FRY GRAVY INGREDIENTS:

- One-quarter cup low-sodium soy sauce
- 2 tbsp rice wine vinegar
- 2 tbsp oyster sauce
- 2 tsps toasted sesame oil
- half tsp ground ginger
- if you want: 1-3 tsps chili garlic sauce, to taste

INSTRUCTIONS

TO PREPARE THE <u>CHICKEN</u> NOODLE STIR-FRY:

1. Cook noodles therefore to package instructions. Drain and put aside.

2. In a <u>large fry pan</u>, warmth one **tbsp** oil over average-high heat. place <u>chicken</u> and spice evenly with a generous pinch of salt and pepper. prepare the <u>chicken</u>, mixing and flipping sometimes, for till this is simply prepared through and no longer pink on the inside (approximately 3-5 mins). Place <u>chicken</u> with a slotted spoon to a else plate, and put aside.

3. Add the remaining two **tbsp** oil to the fry pan, and increase warmth to high. place broccoli, carrots, bell pepper and mushrooms, and fry for 5 mins, either till they reach your desired level of softness.

4. Add within the collard greens, <u>sauce</u>, prepared <u>chicken</u>, noodles, and instantly toss to mix. Keep cooking for two mins, mixing frequently, till the greens have wilted a bit.

5. Take away from warmth and submit immediately, garnished with your desired toppings.

TO PREPARE THE STIR-FRY <u>SAUCE</u>:

1. Whisk all ingredients along till mixd. Then blend in as much chili garlic gravy as you'd like.

NOTES

*You could really employsimply approximately any mushrooms here —— baby bella, white key, shiitakes, either a combination!

**Feel free to sub in whatever greens you have on hand here —— fresh spinach, kale, chard, either mustard greens.

BEEF AND BROCCOLI

- *PREP TIME:* **15 MINS**

- *PREPARE TIME:* **15 MINS**

- *TOTAL TIME:* **30 MINS**

- *YIELD:* **4 -6 SUBMITTINGS**

INGREDIENTS

BEEF AND BROCCOLI INGREDIENTS:

- 1 pound flank steak, slice in One-quarter-inch-thick bite-sized pieces
- 1 tbsp soy sauce
- 1 tbsp rice wine vinegar
- 3–4 cups sliced broccoli florets (approximately one average head of broccoli)
- 1 batch of gravy (see below)
- 1 tbsp peanut oil
- 2 cloves garlic, peeled and minced
- *if you want garnishes:* toasted sesame seeds and/or thinly-sliced green onions

Sauce **Ingredients:**
- three-quarters cup water
- 3 tbsp oyster sauce
- 3 tbsp soy sauce
- 1 tbsp cornstarch
- 1 tbsp rice wine vinegar
- 1 tsp sesame oil
- One-quarter tsp ground ginger
- One-quarter tsp freshly-ground black pepper
- *if you want:* 1-3 tsps sriracha, to taste

TO PREPARE THE BEEF AND BROCCOLI:

1. Add the steak to a big bowl, along with the soy gravy and rice wine vinegar. Stir to mix, then allow the steak marinate for at least ten mins (or up to one hour).

2. Meanwhereas, fill a big stockpot halfway full of water, and bring this to a boil. Stir the broccoli florets in the water, and prepare for 30-45 seconds. Drain (or Place the broccoli to a strainer), and put aside.

3. Prepare the gravy (see instructions below).

4. As the steak has finished marinating, place the peanut oil to a big fry pan either wok over average-high heat. place the steak and garlic, and fry — mixing sometimes — till the steak is prepared through, approximately 5-6 mins. place the gravy and broccoli, and toss to mix. Keep cooking for 1-2 more mins, either till the gravy comes to a simmer and thickens.

5. Take away from warmth and submit immediately, topped with if you want garnishes supposing desired.

TO PREPARE THE SAUCE:

1. Whisk all ingredients along till mixd.

20-MINUTE TERIYAKI <u>*CHICKEN*</u>

- *PREP TIME:* **8 MINS**

- *PREPARE TIME:* **12 MINS**

- *TOTAL TIME:* **20 MINS**

- *YIELD:* **TWO -3 SUBMITTINGS**

INGREDIENTS

20-MINUTE TERIYAKI <u>CHICKEN</u> INGREDIENTS:

- 1 pound boneless skinless <u>chicken</u> breasts, slice in bite-sized pieces
- salt and pepper
- 1 tbsp peanut oil (or any cooking oil)
- 1 batch teriyaki gravy (see below)
- if you want toppings: toasted sesame seeds, thinly-sliced green onions

TERIYAKI GRAVY INGREDIENTS:

- 1 clove garlic, peeled and minced
- One-quarter cup soy <u>sauce</u>
- 2 tbsp honey
- 2 tbsp mirin (sweet rice wine)
- 2 tbsp rice wine vinegar
- 1 tbsp cornstarch
- half tsp sesame oil
- One-quarter tsp ground ginger

INSTRUCTIONS

TO PREPARE THE 20-MINUTE TERIYAKI <u>CHICKEN</u>:

1. Spice the <u>chicken</u> with a several generous pinches of salt and pepper. put aside.

2. In a big fry pan either wok, warmth oil over average-high heat. place <u>chicken</u> and saute, mixing sometimes, till the <u>chicken</u> is prepared through and no longer pink on the inside.

3. Meanwhereas, as the <u>chicken</u> is cooking, prepare your teriyaki <u>sauce</u>.

4. As the <u>chicken</u> is ready to go, pour the teriyaki gravy over it, then toss to mix till the <u>chicken</u> is evenly coated. Keep cooking till the gravy reaches a simmer and thickens.

5. Take away from heat, and submit immediately, garnished with if you want toppings supposing desired.

TO PREPARE THE TERIYAKI <u>SAUCE</u>:

1. Whisk all ingredients along till mixd.

SESAME NOODLES WITH BROCCOLI AND ALMONDS

- *PREP TIME:* 6 MINS

- *PREPARE TIME:* 14 MINS

- *TOTAL TIME:* 20 MINS

- *YIELD:* 6 -8 SUBMITTINGS

INGREDIENTS

SESAME NOODLES WITH BROCCOLI AND ALMONDS INGREDIENTS:

- 1 pound (16 oz.) unprepared linguine (or any noodles, such as rice noodles, soba noodles, lo mein noodles, etc.)
- 1 tbsp peanut either vegetable oil
- 3—4 cups sliced broccoli florets (approximately one average head of broccoli)
- 4 cloves garlic, peeled and thinly-sliced
- salt and pepper
- half cup sliced Blue Diamond Almonds (I used the Wasabi and Soy Sauce variety)
- 1 batch Sesame-Soy Vinaigrette (see below)
- if you want garnishes: thinly-sliced green onions, toasted sesame seeds, coarsely-ground black pepper, crushed red pepper flakes

SESAME-SOY VINAIGRETTE INGREDIENTS:
- One-quarter cup soy sauce
- 2 tbsp rice wine vinegar
- 1 tbsp sesame oil
- half tsp freshly-cracked black pepper
- half tsp ground ginger
- half tsp sriracha either hot chili oil

INSTRUCTIONS

1. Cook noodles al dente in a big stockpot of salted water therefore to package instructions. Drain, and put aside.

2. Meanwhereas, as the <u>pasta</u> is cooking, warmth oil in a big fry pan over average-high heat. place the broccoli florets and spice with a several pinches of salt and pepper. Saute, mixing as a minute either so, for 4-5 mins till this is slightly charred around the edges and prepared through. Stir within the garlic and keep sauteing for 1-2 mins, mixing frequently, till the garlic is prepared and fragrant. Take away from warmth and put aside.

3. Just as the <u>pasta</u> is drained, comeback this to the big stockpot, and stir within the prepared broccoli and garlic, almonds, and gravy till everything is evenly mixd.

4. Serve immediately, topped with your desired garnishes. either refrigerate the noodles in a sealed container for up to 3 days. (This dish is also awesome just as served chilled.)

1. Whisk all ingredients along till mixd. put aside.

PAD SEE EW

- *PREP TIME:* TEN MINS

- *PREPARE TIME:* TEN MINS

- *TOTAL TIME:* 20 MINS

- *YIELD:* 4 SUBMITTINGS

INGREDIENTS

STIR-FRY INGREDIENTS:

- 12 ounces (dry) rice stick noodles
- 2 Tbsp peanut either vegetable oil, divided
- 1 pound boneless skinless chicken breasts, slice in bite-sized pieces*
- 5 cups (packed) Chinese broccoli, sliced in bite-sized pieces with the stems and leaves separated
- 3 cloves garlic, peeled and minced
- 2 eggs, whisked
- stir-fry gravy (see below)
- (if you want: fried garlic, lime wedges, for submitting)

STIR-FRY SAUCE:

- 3 Tablespooons *dark* sweet soy sauce
- 1 Tbsp oyster sauce
- 1 Tbsp (regular) soy sauce
- 1 Tbsp rice wine vinegar
- 2–3 tsps sugar either honey
- *if you want*: 1-2 tsps chili garlic sauce, to taste

1. Prepare noodles al dente therefore to package instructions. (Or supposing there are no instructions, I advised placing the noodles in a big mixing bowl and pouring boiling water on top of them till they are submerged. Wait 3-5 mins till they are soft and al dente, then drain the water and set the noodles aside till ready to use, breaking them up with your fingers so that they don't stick along.)

2. Meanwhereas, warmth **one Tbsp oil** in a big fry pan either wok over high heat. Stir within the <u>chicken</u> and Chinese broccoli stems and garlic and prepare for 4-6 mins, flipping and mixing sometimes, till the <u>chicken</u> is simply prepared through. (The <u>chicken</u> should be no longer be pink on the inside.) Place the mix to a else plate and put aside.

3. Add one **tsp** of the remaining oil to the fry pan either wok. place the eggs, and quickly scramble them, mixing sometimes, till they are cooked. (Alternately, you'll also scramble the eggs beforehand and put aside till ready to use, either prepare them simultaneously in another fry pan, supposing your current pan isn't big enough.)

4. Add within the remaining two **tsps** oil, the prepared noodles, <u>chicken</u> and broccoli stems, broccoli leaves, stir-fry <u>sauce</u>, and give the mix a good toss till everything is mixd. Keep cooking for 2-3 more mins, tossing frequently. Taste, and spice with salt and pepper supposing needed.

5. Serve immediately, with if you want garnishes supposing desired.

1. Whisk all ingredients along till mixd. Supposing you'd like to place in some heat, place in 1-2 tsps chili garlic gravy to taste.

NOTES

*Feel free to substitute in one pound of steak, shrimp, pork, either tofu in place of the <u>chicken</u>. Simply fry till this is prepared through, and proceed with the rest of the recipe as instructed.

Printed in Great Britain
by Amazon

10195771R00036